"The Wealth Code: Unlocking the Secrets to Making Money"

By Jasmine Dudley

Cover design by DP HOUSE MEDIA

Interior design by DP HOUSE MEDIA

Published by: Dudley Publishing House

ISBN 9798987671504

Printed in USA

First edition 2023

Contact Author : Bit.ly/coachjasminedudley

DP HOUSE

Dudley Publishing House

www.dudleypublishinghouse.net

Dedication

This book is dedicated to all the individuals who are striving to achieve financial freedom and reach their financial goals. May the insights and strategies shared within these pages serve as a guide and inspiration to start you on your journey towards wealth and success.

Special Dedication: In loving memory of

James Lee Dudley

My Father in Love! They often say I have a brain like yours. You were one of the most brilliant brains I had ever encountered in my life. You would sit us in the living room and come up with 10 different businesses EVERYDAY and the strategies to scale them to millions effortlessly. The greatest legacy I will ever inherit...The gift of your brain. I dedicate this book to you! I love you and miss you Daddy!

"The Wealth Code: Unlocking the Secrets to Building and Maintaining Wealth" is a must-read guide for anyone looking to build and maintain wealth. Written by a financial expert, this book delves into the essential strategies and principles needed to achieve financial success. From understanding the basics of credit scores and debt management, to investing in real estate, stock market and building a strong financial foundation, this book provides a comprehensive guide to building wealth through various means. It also provides practical tips and advice on how to stay on track and maintain financial success over the long term. "The Wealth Code" is an invaluable resource for anyone looking to take control of their finances and secure their financial future."

-Coach Jasmine Dudley

Throughout this book I will recommend certain platforms and products. I have made it easy for you to access these products on the next page! Plus, some extra special gifts from me!

All you have to do is scan this code with your mobile phone and it will take you directly to all my recommendations. Think of it as your book companion.

(Can't scan code? Visit Bit.ly/WEALTHCODECOMP)

Table of Content

1- Understanding the Mindset of Wealth 11

2- The Power of Goal Setting and Planning...........19

3- Investing 101: The Basics of Building Wealth.....25

4- Real Estate Investing:

   The Path to Financial Freedom......................33

5- Stock Market Strategies for Making Money........39

6- Building a Business: From Idea to Profit...........45

7- Building a Strong Online Presence for Your

   Business...53

8- Networking for Success:

   Building Connections to Grow Your Wealth.......65

9- Building and Managing a Credit Score:

   Personal and Business...............................69

10- Retirement Planning:

   Securing Your Financial Future.....................79

11- Building a Strong Financial Foundation............85

12- Putting it All Together and Staying on Track for

   Financial Success....................................89

13- (Bonus) 10 Side Hustles That You Can Turn Into Businesses...…..…97

About the Author....................................…...103

1

Understanding the Mindset of Wealth

Welcome to The Wealth Code: Unlocking the Secrets to Making Money." In this book, we will explore the various strategies and techniques that successful individuals use to build and maintain wealth. We will delve into the mindset, habits, and actions that are necessary to achieve financial success.

Before we begin, it's important to understand that wealth is not just about having a lot of money. It's about having the freedom and security to live the life you want. It's about having the resources to pursue your passions, take care of your loved ones, and make a positive impact on the world.

In order to achieve wealth, you must first change your mindset. Many people believe that wealth is something that only a select few can attain, that it's reserved for the lucky or the elite. But the truth is that anyone can become wealthy if they are willing to put in the work and make the right choices.

A wealth mindset refers to an attitude and set of beliefs that are conducive to building and maintaining wealth. This can include beliefs such as the value of hard work, the importance of financial education and planning, and the potential for growth and abundance. It also includes a willingness to take calculated risks and the ability to delay immediate gratification in pursuit of long-term financial goals. People with a wealth mindset often have a positive and proactive approach to money, view money as a tool to be used to achieve their goals, and are committed to constant self-improvement and learning in the area of personal finance.

The key to changing your mindset is to understand that wealth is not something that happens to you, it's something that you create. Deuteronomy 8:18 says "And you shall remember the LORD your God, for it is He who gives you the power to get wealth…" Many people make the mistake of thinking that wealth is something that will just drop in your lap from God.

Many people are overcome with the fear of wealth that hinders their ability to prosper. There are several reasons why some people may be afraid of wealth. One reason is past experiences or traumas related to money. For example, if someone grew up in a household where money was scarce, they may associate wealth with negative experiences and struggle to feel comfortable with the idea of having more money.

Here are other reasons why people may be afraid of wealth:

1) Fear of change: Acquiring wealth can bring significant change to one's life, including changes in lifestyle, relationships, and responsibilities. This can be overwhelming and scary for some people.

2) Fear of losing it: Once a person has acquired wealth, they may be afraid of losing it, either through poor investment decisions, fraud, or market fluctuations.

3) Fear of responsibility: Wealth can come with a sense of responsibility, such as the responsibility to invest it wisely, to use it for good causes, and to manage it effectively. This can be daunting for some people.

4) Fear of criticism: Some people may be afraid of how others will perceive them, or fear criticism and judgement from friends, family, and society, for being wealthy.

5) Fear of not deserving it: Some people may feel guilty or undeserving of wealth, due to past experiences, upbringing, or societal messages that wealth is only for a select few.

6) Fear of the unknown: Many people may not have had much exposure to wealth and may be uncertain about how to handle it, manage it, and make it grow.

7) Fear of losing oneself: Some people may be afraid of losing their sense of identity, values, and purpose, as they acquire wealth, especially if they have been raised with a certain set of values.

8) Fear of being different: Fear of standing out, being different and being seen as a "rich person" can lead to not wanting to have wealth.

"The Wealth Code: Unlocking the Secrets to Making Money"

It's important to note that these fears are not necessarily rational, and often stem from past experiences, limiting beliefs, and societal messages. By identifying and addressing these fears, people can learn to overcome them and develop a healthier relationship with money and wealth.

Here are a few ways to help overcome a fear of wealth:

1) Identify the root cause: Often, a fear of wealth can stem from past experiences or beliefs. Identifying the underlying cause of your fear can help you understand and address it.

2) Educate yourself: Lack of knowledge about money and wealth can contribute to a fear of it. Educating yourself on personal finance, investing, and wealth-building strategies can help you feel more confident and in control.

3) Reframe your thoughts: Instead of focusing on the negative aspects of wealth, try to reframe your thoughts and focus on the positive impact that wealth can have on your life and the lives of others.

[15]

4) Surround yourself with positive influences: Surround yourself with people who have a healthy relationship with money and wealth. They can serve as positive role models and provide support and guidance.

5) Practice mindfulness: Fear can often manifest as physical symptoms such as anxiety and stress. Mindfulness practices such as, change of scenery, meditation & prayer, and taking a moment to just breathe can help you manage these symptoms.

6) Take action: One of the best ways to overcome fear is to take action. Start small by setting financial goals and working towards them. As you start to see progress, you'll feel more confident and less fearful.

7) Remember that change in mindset is a continuous process, it may take time and patience to overcome this fear but with the right approach and mindset you can take control of your financial life and build wealth.

In this book, we will explore the different ways that you can create wealth, including investing, building a business, and maximizing your income. We will also discuss the common pitfalls and mistakes that people make on their journey to wealth, and provide strategies for avoiding them.

As you read and learn, always remember that wealth is not about having more money than you need, it's about having enough money to live the life you want. With the right mindset and the right strategies, you can achieve financial success and live the life of your dreams.

STOP: What have you learned so far? Use this section to jot down notes.

2

The Power of Goal Setting and Planning

One of the most important steps on the path to wealth is setting clear and specific goals. Without a clear understanding of what you want to achieve, it's impossible to create a plan to get there. Goals give you direction and focus, and provide the motivation you need to keep moving forward.

In this chapter, we will discuss the importance of goal setting and planning for achieving wealth. We will explore the different types of goals you can set and provide strategies for creating a plan to achieve them. We will also discuss the benefits of having a plan, including the ability to track progress, stay motivated, and make informed decisions.

Goal setting and planning are powerful tools for achieving wealth, but they are only effective if you take consistent and persistent action. It's important to remember that success is not a destination, it's a journey, and the key to success is to stay focused and take action every day.

The first step in goal setting is to identify what you truly want. This can be challenging as many people have a tendency to set goals based on what they think they should want, rather than what they truly desire. To set effective goals, you must be honest with yourself about what you want to achieve.

Once you've identified your goals, the next step is to make them specific and measurable. For example, instead of saying "I want to be rich," say "I want to have a net worth of $5 million in the next 5 years." This specific goal gives you a clear target to work towards and a way to measure your progress.

In addition to setting specific goals, it's important to set both short-term and long-term goals. Short-term goals are those that can be achieved in a relatively short period of time, such as saving a certain amount of money in the next 6 months. Long-term goals are those that will take longer to achieve, such as reaching a certain net worth in the next 10 years.

It's also important to make sure your goals are SMART: Specific, Measurable, Achievable, Realistic, and Time-bound. This means that your goals should be clearly defined, with a specific target, a deadline for achieving it, and a plan for how to get there.

Here are some steps to creating S.M.A.R.T goals:

1) Specific: Clearly define what you want to achieve. Be specific about what you want to accomplish, and make sure your goal is clearly defined and measurable.

2) Measurable: Set specific criteria for measuring progress towards your goal. Include quantifiable elements such as numbers, dates, and percentages.

3) Achievable: Make sure your goal is realistic and achievable. Consider any constraints or obstacles that you may face, and develop a plan to overcome them.

4) Relevant: Ensure that your goal is relevant to your overall life and financial objectives, and that it aligns with your values and priorities.

5) Time-bound: Set a deadline for achieving your goal. This will help you stay focused and motivated, and give you a sense of urgency to work towards your goal.

6) Write it down: Write down your goal in a visible place, so that you can see it every day and keep it at the forefront of your mind.

7) Break it down: Break down your goal into smaller, more manageable steps. This will make the goal feel less overwhelming, and give you a clear plan of action.

8) Get Support: Share your goal with someone you trust, who can provide you with support and accountability.

9) Review and adjust: Regularly review your progress and adjust your plan as needed. Celebrate your successes and learn from your setbacks.

Once you have set your goals, the next step is to develop a plan for achieving them. This might include creating a budget, developing a savings plan, or researching investment options. It's important to have a clear understanding of what steps you need to take and the resources you will need to reach your goals.

Creating a plan also means that you will have to make some sacrifices. You may have to cut back on your expenses or put in extra hours at work in order to achieve your financial goals. But by having a clear plan, you will be able to stay focused and motivated and make progress toward your objectives.

Remember, setting goals and creating a plan is the foundation for achieving wealth. By taking the time to set clear and specific goals and develop a plan for achieving them, you will be well on your way to financial success.

In this chapter, we've discussed the importance of goal setting and planning in the process of creating wealth. In the next chapters, we will explore different strategies and techniques for achieving your goals and building wealth.

STOP: What have you learned so far? Use this section to jot down notes.

3

Investing 101: The Basics of Building Wealth

Investing is one of the most powerful ways to build wealth over time. By investing your money, you can earn a return that outpaces inflation, allowing your money to grow and compound over time.

Before you start investing, it's important to understand the different types of investments available to you. Some common types of investments include stocks, bonds, mutual funds, real estate, and alternative investments like cryptocurrency. Each of these types of investments has its own set of risks and potential rewards, and it's important to understand the basics of how they work before you start putting your money into them.

One of the most important concepts to understand when it comes to investing is risk vs reward. The more risk you are willing to take on, the higher the potential reward.

REWIND: The more risk you are willing to take on, the higher the potential reward.

However, it's also important to remember that higher risk investments also come with a higher potential for loss. As you start investing, it's important to find a balance between risk and reward that is comfortable for you.

Another important concept to understand is diversification. Diversification means spreading your money across different types of investments, in order to reduce risk. By diversifying your portfolio, you can reduce the impact of any one investment on your overall portfolio.

In this chapter, we will discuss the basics of investing, including the different types of investments available, the concept of risk vs reward, and the importance of diversification. We will also provide strategies for getting started with investing, including setting investment goals, developing a plan, and finding the right investment options for you.

Remember, investing is a key component of building wealth over time. By understanding the basics of investing and developing a plan for investing your money, you can put your money to work for you and achieve your financial goals.

Investing is the process of putting money into assets with the expectation of earning a return. There are many different types of investments, each with their own unique characteristics, risks, and potential returns.

Here some examples of things to invest in:

1) Stocks: Investing in stocks means buying shares of ownership in a publicly traded company. Stocks can provide the potential for high returns, but also come with higher risk.

2) Bonds: Investing in bonds means lending money to a government or corporation. Bonds generally have lower returns than stocks but also come with less risk.

3) Mutual Funds and ETFs: These are professionally managed investment portfolios that pool money from many investors to buy a diversified mix of stocks, bonds, or other assets. They offer a convenient way for small investors to get diversified exposure to the market.

4) Real Estate: Investing in real estate involves buying, owning, renting and/or selling property. Real estate can provide a steady stream of income through rent, but also comes with higher costs and potential for illiquidity.

5) Commodities: Investing in commodities such as gold, silver, oil, or agricultural products can provide a hedge against inflation and market fluctuations.

6) Cryptocurrencies: Investing in cryptocurrencies such as Bitcoin and Ethereum is a relatively new and highly speculative way to invest, with a high degree of volatility.

Before investing, it's important to consider your personal financial situation, risk tolerance, and investment goals. It's also important to do your own research and consult with a financial advisor before making any investment decisions.

Getting started with investing in stocks can seem daunting, but it doesn't have to be.

Here are a few steps to help you get started:

1) Educate yourself: Learn about the basics of stock investing, including how stock markets work, the

different types of stocks, and the risks and potential returns involved.

2) Assess your risk tolerance: Before investing in stocks, consider your risk tolerance and investment goals. Stocks can be volatile and come with higher risk than other types of investments, so it's important to be comfortable with the level of risk you are taking on.

3) Open a brokerage account: To buy and sell stocks, you will need to open a brokerage account. There are many online brokerage firms that offer easy and low-cost ways to invest in stocks.

4) Decide on your investment strategy: There are many different ways to invest in stocks, such as buying individual stocks, investing in exchange-traded funds (ETFs) or mutual funds, or using a robo-advisor. Consider which strategy aligns best with your goals and risk tolerance.

5) Diversify: Diversifying your portfolio is an important aspect of investing, it means spreading

your investments across different types of assets, sectors and companies. This can help reduce risk and increase your chances of earning a positive return over the long term.

6) Start small: It's okay to start small and invest a small amount of money at first. As you become more comfortable with the process and learn more about investing, you can gradually increase your investment.

7) Monitor and adjust: Keep an eye on your investments and monitor their performance. If necessary, make adjustments to your portfolio to ensure it aligns with your investment goals and risk tolerance.

Remember, investing in stocks is a long-term commitment, it's important to stay informed, diversify and be patient with your investments. It's also important to consult with a financial advisor before making any investment decisions.

One personal lesson that you may have learned from this chapter is the importance of setting investment goals. By setting clear and specific goals, you can give direction and purpose to your investing efforts and measure your progress and success.

Another lesson that you may have learned is the importance of balance between risk and reward. As you start investing, it's important to find a balance between risk and reward that is comfortable for you, understanding that the more risk you take the higher the potential reward, but also the potential for loss.

You may also have learned about the importance of diversification and spreading your money across different types of investments in order to reduce risk in your portfolio.

Finally, you may have learned the importance of developing a plan for investing your money, including setting investment goals, researching investment options, and monitoring your progress. By understanding the basics of investing and developing a plan, you can put your money to work for you and achieve your financial goals.

STOP: What have you learned so far? Use this section to jot down notes.

4

Real Estate Investing: The Path to Financial Freedom

Real estate investing can be a powerful tool for building wealth and achieving financial freedom. It's one of the few investments that can provide a steady stream of income, as well as the potential for long-term appreciation.

When it comes to real estate investing, there are several different strategies to choose from, such as buying rental properties, flipping houses, or investing in commercial properties. Each strategy has its own set of risks and potential rewards, and it's important to understand the basics of how they work before you start putting your money into them.

One of the most important concepts to understand when it comes to real estate investing is cash flow. Cash flow is the money you have left over after paying all of your expenses on a property. Positive cash flow means that you are earning more money from a property than you are spending, while negative cash flow means that you are spending more money than you are earning.

Another important concept to understand is leverage. Leverage allows you to control a property worth much more than the amount of money you have invested. This can increase your potential returns, but also increases your risk.

In this chapter, we will discuss the basics of real estate investing, including the different strategies available, the concept of cash flow, and the importance of leverage. We will also provide strategies for getting started with real estate investing, including setting investment goals, researching different markets, and finding the right properties for you.

Remember, real estate investing can be a powerful tool for building wealth and achieving financial freedom. By understanding the basics of real estate investing and developing a plan, you can put your money to work for you in the real estate market and achieve your financial goals.

Airbnb has become a popular form of real estate investing in recent years, as it allows individuals to rent out their properties on a short-term basis to travelers.

One strategy for Airbnb real estate investing is to purchase a property specifically for the purpose of renting it out on Airbnb. This might include a vacation home or a property in a tourist-friendly location. By purchasing a property in an area with high demand for short-term rentals, investors can potentially see a high return on their investment.

Another strategy is to invest in a turn-key property, which is a property that is already set up and ready to be rented out on Airbnb. This type of investment can save the investor time and money, as the property is already prepared for short-term rental.

Additionally, it's important to keep in mind the laws and regulations of the area you're investing in, as some cities and states have specific laws and regulations for short-term rentals and Airbnb properties. It's important to research and comply with these regulations to avoid any legal issues.

Airbnb real estate investing can be a great way to generate passive income and build wealth. By understanding the market demand, researching properties and laws, and developing a plan, investors can tap into the potential of the Airbnb market and achieve their financial goals.

Securing an Airbnb through a corporate lease is a strategy that allows investors to rent out their properties on a short-term basis while also protecting themselves legally and financially.

One way to secure an Airbnb through a corporate lease is to set up a separate legal entity, such as a limited liability company (LLC), to act as the tenant. This LLC would be the entity responsible for the lease agreement, and would also be the entity responsible for any damages or disputes that may arise during the tenancy.

A corporate lease is a lease agreement between a landlord and a corporation, rather than an individual. By entering into a corporate lease, the landlord can protect themselves from liability and financial losses that may occur as a result of renting out the property on Airbnb.

Another strategy is to work with a property management company that specializes in corporate leasing for Airbnb properties. These companies typically handle the legal and financial aspects of the lease, and can also manage the property and handle bookings.

It's also important to note that some landlords require a higher security deposit, additional insurance, and/or a corporate guarantee from the tenant. This can provide additional protection for the landlord in case of any damages or disputes that may occur during the tenancy.

Overall, securing an Airbnb through a corporate lease can provide additional legal and financial protection for landlords while still allowing them to rent out their properties on a short-term basis. By setting up a separate legal entity or working with a property management company that specializes in corporate leasing, landlords can protect themselves while still tapping into the potential of the Airbnb market.

There are several other ways to invest in real estate, including:

1) Buying rental properties: This involves purchasing a property and renting it out to tenants. This can provide a steady stream of rental income, as well as potential appreciation in the value of the property over time.

2) Fix-and-flip: This involves buying a property, making repairs and renovations, and then selling it for a profit. This can be a riskier strategy, but can also provide significant returns if done correctly.

3) REITs (Real Estate Investment Trusts): REITs allow investors to invest in a diversified portfolio of properties, without the need to own or manage the properties themselves. They can be a more passive way to invest in real estate.

4) Crowdfunding: Platforms like Fundrise and RealtyMogul allow investors to pool their money together to invest in larger real estate projects.

5) Private lending: Private lending refers to lending money to real estate investors or developers to finance their projects. It can provide a higher return on investment compared to traditional fixed-income investments.

These are some of the most common ways to invest in real estate, however, it's important to do your own research and consult with professionals to find the best option for your financial situation and investment goals.

5

Stock Market Strategies for Making Money

T he stock market can be a powerful tool for making money, but it's important to understand the basics of how it works and the different strategies for investing in stocks.

Before you start investing in the stock market, it's important to understand the different types of stocks available, such as common stocks, preferred stocks, and exchange-traded funds (ETFs). Each of these types of stocks has its own set of risks and potential rewards, and it's important to understand the basics of how they work before you start putting your money into them.

One of the most important concepts to understand when it comes to investing in the stock market is risk vs reward. The more risk you are willing to take on, the higher the potential reward. However, it's also important to remember that higher risk investments also come with a higher potential for loss. As you start investing, it's important to find a balance between risk and reward that is comfortable for you.

Another important concept to understand is diversification. Diversification means spreading your money across different types of stocks and sectors, in order to reduce risk. By diversifying your portfolio, you can reduce the impact of any one stock on your overall portfolio.

In this chapter, we will discuss different stock market strategies, such as value investing, growth investing, and dividend investing. We will also discuss the importance of conducting research and due diligence before investing in any stock.

In addition, we will talk about the importance of monitoring and adjusting your portfolio, as market conditions and individual stocks can change over time.

Remember, the stock market can be a powerful tool for making money, but it's important to understand the basics of how it works and the different strategies for investing in stocks. By understanding the concepts of risk vs reward, diversification, and conducting research, you can make informed decisions and potentially achieve your financial goals through stock market investments.

NFTs, or non-fungible tokens, are digital assets that are unique and cannot be replicated or replaced. They are used to represent ownership of a digital asset, such as artwork, music, videos, and other forms of digital content.

There are several ways to make money through NFTs, one of them is by creating and selling your own NFTs. This can include digital artwork, music, videos, and other forms of digital content. By creating unique and valuable NFTs, you can potentially sell them for a high price to collectors and investors who are interested in owning one-of-a-kind digital assets.

Another way to make money through NFTs is by buying and reselling them. Similar to traditional art or collectible markets, some NFTs can appreciate in value over time. By buying NFTs at a lower price and reselling them at a higher price, you can make a profit. However, it's important to note that the value of NFTs can be highly speculative and subject to market conditions, so it's important to conduct research and due diligence before buying any NFTs.

Additionally, you can also make money through NFTs by participating in NFT marketplaces, platforms or communities where people can buy, sell, bid, and discover NFTs. These platforms typically take a percentage of the sale as commission, but they also provide a marketplace and tools to showcase your NFTs and reach potential buyers.

It's important to note that the NFT market is still relatively new and highly speculative, and it's important to conduct research and due diligence before investing any money in NFTs. It's also important to be aware of the legal and regulatory environment of NFTs, as laws and regulations may vary from country to country.

Overall, NFTs can be a way to make money by creating, buying, and reselling unique digital assets, but it's important to understand the market and the risks involved before jumping into it.

Getting started with NFTs can seem intimidating at first, but it's not as difficult as it may seem.

Here are a few steps you can take to get started:

1) Research: Before diving into the world of NFTs, it's important to do your research. Learn about the different types of NFTs available and the different platforms where you can buy, sell, and create them. Research the artists and creators who are currently making a name for themselves in the NFT market.

2) Choose a platform: Decide where you want to buy, sell, or create your NFTs. There are several platforms available such as OpenSea, Rarible, SuperRare, and

"The Wealth Code: Unlocking the Secrets to Making Money"

Nifty Gateway, each with their own unique features and community.

3) Create a wallet: In order to buy, sell, or create NFTs, you'll need to have a digital wallet that supports Ethereum, the blockchain network on which most NFTs are built. Some popular options include MetaMask, MyEtherWallet, and Coinbase Wallet.

4) Get some Ether: In order to buy, sell, or create NFTs, you'll need some Ether, the cryptocurrency used to pay for transactions on the Ethereum network. You can purchase Ether on a cryptocurrency exchange like Coinbase, Binance, or Kraken.

5) Start buying, selling, or creating: Once you have a wallet set up and some Ether, you can start buying, selling, or creating NFTs. When buying, look for NFTs that you like and that you think have potential.

STOP: What have you learned so far? Use this section to jot down notes.

6

Building a Business: From Idea to Profit

Building a successful business can be one of the most powerful ways to achieve financial success. Starting a business allows you to be your own boss, set your own schedule, and earn a potentially unlimited income.

Before starting a business, it's important to do your research and develop a solid business plan. This includes identifying a target market, developing a unique value proposition, and outlining a marketing and sales strategy. It's also important to understand the financial aspects of running a business, including budgeting, cash flow management, and taxation.

One important aspect of building a business is finding the right idea or niche. This means identifying a problem or need in the market and developing a solution or service that meets that need. It's also important to validate your idea by researching and testing it with potential customers.

Another important aspect is to have a clear financial plan for your business, including budgeting, forecasting, and cash flow management. This will help you to understand the financial health of your business, and make informed decisions on how to grow and improve it.

In addition, it's important to have a strong team and a solid network to support your business. This includes hiring the right employees, building a team of advisors and mentors, and networking with other entrepreneurs and industry experts.

In this chapter, we will discuss the key elements of building a successful business, including idea validation, financial planning, and building a team. We will also provide strategies for getting started, including developing a business plan and finding the right resources and support.

Building a legal business involves a number of steps to ensure that your business is compliant with all relevant laws and regulations.

Here are a few steps you can take to ensure that your business is legal:

1) Choose a business structure: Decide on the type of business structure that best suits your needs, such as a sole proprietorship, partnership, limited liability company (LLC), or corporation. Each structure has its own set of legal and financial implications, so it's important to consult with a lawyer or accountant before making a decision.

2) Register your business: Register your business with the appropriate state and local agencies. This may include obtaining a business license and registering for taxes.

3) Obtain any necessary permits and licenses: Depending on the type of business you are running, you may need to obtain specific permits and licenses. For example, businesses that serve food or alcohol, or businesses that provide certain services, may need to obtain specific permits or licenses.

4) Comply with employment laws: Make sure that your business is in compliance with all relevant

employment laws, including those related to hiring, firing, and employee benefits.

5) Protect your intellectual property: If your business involves any unique ideas, products, or designs, it's important to protect your intellectual property by filing for patents, trademarks, or copyrights.

6) Obtain insurance: Obtain the necessary insurance to protect your business and your employees from potential liabilities.

7) Understand consumer protection laws: Make sure that you understand and comply with consumer protection laws, including those related to advertising, pricing, and refunds.

8) Keep accurate records: Keep accurate records of all financial transactions, including income and expenses, and ensure that your business is compliant with all relevant tax laws.

It's important to note that laws and regulations may vary depending on the jurisdiction and type of business, so it's important to consult with a lawyer or accountant to ensure that your business is fully compliant with all relevant laws and regulations.

Validating a business idea is the process of testing and confirming that there is a market need for your product or service and that it can generate a profitable revenue stream. **Here are some steps you can take to validate your business idea:**

1) Conduct Market Research: Understand your target market, competitors, and industry trends. This information will help you to identify opportunities and potential challenges for your business idea.

2) Speak to Potential Customers: Reach out to potential customers and ask for their feedback on your business idea. Understand their pain points and how your product or service addresses them.

3) Create a Minimum Viable Product (MVP): Develop a basic version of your product or service and test it with a small group of customers. This will help you to understand how your product or service performs in the market and make adjustments accordingly.

4) Use Online Surveys and Polls: Use online tools to survey a larger group of potential customers and gather feedback on your business idea.

5) Test Your Business Model: Run a small pilot test of your business model to understand the costs and revenue potential of your business idea.

6) Look for Indicator of Interest: Look for signs of interest from potential customers, such as pre-orders or waitlists, which can indicate a strong demand for your product or service.

7) Consider hiring a consultant: They can provide you with valuable insights and knowledge to improve your business idea and validate it by using their market and industry expertise.

It's important to keep in mind that validating a business idea is an ongoing process and requires constant feedback, testing, and iteration. It's also important to be open to pivot or change your business idea based on market feedback and validation results.

Financial planning for a business involves creating a comprehensive plan for managing the financial aspects of the business, including forecasting revenue and expenses, managing cash flow, and setting financial goals. Here are some steps you can take to create a financial plan for your business:

1) Create a budget: A budget is a financial plan that helps you to forecast your revenue and expenses. It is essential for keeping your business financially stable and helps you to make informed decisions about spending.

2) Develop a cash flow forecast: A cash flow forecast will help you to predict when your business will have more or less cash available. This is crucial for managing cash flow and ensuring that your business has enough money to meet its short-term needs.

3) Create a financial forecast: A financial forecast will help you to predict your business's financial performance over a period of time. This will help you to identify trends and make adjustments to your financial plan accordingly.

4) Set financial goals: Setting financial goals will help you to focus your efforts and measure your progress.

These goals should be specific, measurable, achievable, relevant, and time-bound.

5) Review your financial plan regularly: Reviewing your financial plan regularly will help you to stay on track and make adjustments as needed. This will help you to identify potential issues and make changes before they become a problem.

6) Seek professional advice: A financial advisor or accountant can provide valuable advice and guidance on financial planning for your business. They can help you to understand financial statements, tax laws, and other financial matters, and can provide valuable insights into your business's financial health.

7) Implement financial management systems: Implementing financial management systems, such as accounting software, can help you to keep track of your business's financial performance and make data-driven decisions.

By following these steps, you can create a comprehensive and effective financial plan for your business that will help you to achieve your financial goals and ensure long-term success.

7

Building a Strong Online Presence for Your Business

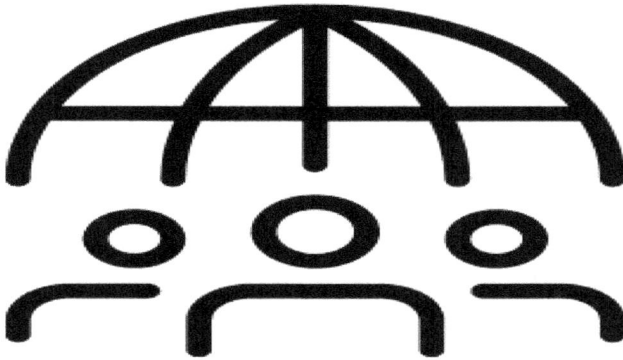

In today's digital age, having a strong online presence is essential for any business. A well-designed and optimized website, active social media accounts, funnels, and positive online reviews can help attract new customers and grow your business. In this chapter, we will discuss the importance of building a strong online presence and provide tips and strategies for creating and maintaining a successful online presence for your business. We will cover topics such as:

The importance of having a professional and user-friendly website, how to use social media to connect with customers and promote your business, the importance of online reviews and how to manage them. We'll also touch on using SEO and other digital marketing strategies to increase online visibility and drive traffic to your website and, Tips for creating and executing an effective online marketing campaign. By following the advice outlined in this chapter, you can help your business to establish a strong online presence, reach new customers, and grow your business.

Remember, having a professional and user-friendly website is crucial for any business or individual looking to establish a strong online presence. A well-designed website can help to build trust with potential customers and clients, increase visibility and credibility, and drive sales and revenue.

Here are a few reasons why having a professional and user-friendly website is important:

1. Establishing a strong online presence: A professional and user-friendly website is the foundation of a strong online presence. It can help to establish your brand, build trust with potential customers, and increase visibility and credibility.

2. Improving conversions: A professional and user-friendly website can help to improve conversions by making it easy for visitors to navigate and find what they are looking for. This can lead to more sales and revenue for your business.

3. Enhancing credibility: A professional and user-friendly website can help to enhance credibility by providing visitors with a positive and professional first impression. This can lead to more trust and ultimately more business.

4. Building trust: A professional and user-friendly website can help to build trust with potential customers by providing them with the information they need and making it easy for them to contact you or make a purchase.

5. Providing value: A professional and user-friendly website can help to provide value to visitors by providing them with useful and relevant information. This can lead to more engagement and ultimately more business.

6. Improving search engine optimization (SEO): A professional and user-friendly website can help to improve SEO by making it easy for search engines to crawl and index the site. This can lead to higher search engine rankings and more visibility.

In summary, a professional and user-friendly website is essential for any business or individual looking to establish a strong online presence and drive sales and revenue. It provides a valuable tool for building trust, enhancing credibility, and providing value to visitors, which in turn can lead to more business and revenue.

Social media can be a powerful tool for connecting with customers and promoting your business.

Here are some ways you can use social media to connect with customers and promote your business:

1. Create a social media presence: Create accounts on popular social media platforms such as Facebook, Twitter, Instagram, and LinkedIn. Use these platforms to connect with customers, share content, and promote your business.

2. Use content marketing: Use social media to share valuable and relevant content with your audience. This can include blog posts, infographics, videos,

and other types of content that provide value to your audience.

3. Engage with your audience: Use social media to engage with your audience by responding to comments and messages, running contests, and creating polls. This can help to build a community of loyal customers.

4. Use paid advertising: Use social media advertising to reach a larger audience and drive more traffic to your website. This can include sponsored posts, promoted tweets, and other types of ads.

5. Use analytics: Use social media analytics to track the performance of your social media campaigns and measure the success of your efforts. This can help you to understand which strategies are working and which need to be improved.

6. Use social media to generate leads: Use social media to generate leads by creating lead magnets such as e-books, webinars, and free trials. This can help to convert your followers into customers.

7. Use Influencers: Utilize influencers to promote your business, product or service. Influencer marketing can help you to reach a larger audience and increase brand awareness.

8. Be consistent: Be consistent with your social media presence. Post regularly, engage with your audience, and use the same branding and messaging across all of your social media channels.

By following these strategies, you can use social media to connect with customers, build a community of loyal followers, and promote your business.

Online reviews are important because they can greatly impact the reputation and credibility of a business. Positive reviews can attract new customers, while negative reviews can drive them away.

Here are a few reasons why online reviews are important and how to manage them:

1. Impact on search rankings: Positive reviews can improve a business's search rankings on search engines like Google. This can lead to more visibility and an increase in website traffic.

2. Impact on consumer decision-making: Consumers often rely on online reviews to make purchasing decisions. Positive reviews can lead to increased sales, while negative reviews can lead to lost business.

3. Impact on brand reputation: Positive reviews can enhance a brand's reputation, while negative reviews can damage it.

4. Monitor your reviews: Regularly monitor your reviews by setting up alerts for new reviews, responding to them promptly, and addressing any negative feedback.

5. Respond to reviews: Respond to both positive and negative reviews in a timely manner. Acknowledge the feedback and thank your customers for their support. Address any concerns or complaints and offer solutions.

6. Encourage reviews: Encourage your customers to leave reviews by including links to your review

profiles in your email signature, on your website, and on your social media profiles.

7. Use reviews to improve your business: Use the feedback in reviews to identify areas of improvement and make changes to your business.

8. Be professional: Always respond professionally, even when dealing with negative reviews.

By managing your online reviews, you can use them as a valuable tool to improve your business and build a positive reputation. Here's how:

1. Search engine optimization (SEO) and other digital marketing strategies can help to increase online visibility and drive traffic to your website. Here are some ways you can use SEO and other digital marketing strategies to increase online visibility and drive traffic to your website:

2. Optimize your website for search engines: Optimize your website for search engines by including relevant keywords, meta tags, and alt tags. Make sure your website is mobile-friendly and has a fast-loading speed.

3. Create valuable content: Create valuable and informative content that addresses the needs and interests of your target audience. This can include blog posts, videos, infographics, and other types of content.

4. Build backlinks: Build backlinks to your website by guest blogging, submitting to directories, and getting listed in industry-specific databases.

5. Use social media: Use social media to promote your website, share content, and build relationships with your target audience.

6. Use paid advertising: Use paid advertising to reach a larger audience and drive more traffic to your website. This can include pay-per-click (PPC) advertising, social media advertising, and display advertising.

7. Use analytics: Use analytics tools to track the performance of your digital marketing campaigns and measure the success of your efforts.

8. Optimize for Local SEO: Optimize your website for local SEO by including your business name, address, and phone number (NAP) on your website, and creating listings on online directories such as Google My Business.

9. Create landing pages/ Funnels: Create landing pages that are optimized for conversions and target specific keywords to increase the chances of visitors taking a desired action.

By using SEO and other digital marketing strategies, you can increase online visibility, drive more traffic to your website, and ultimately increase sales and revenue. It's important to note that SEO and digital marketing are ongoing process and require regular attention, testing and optimization.

Tips for creating and executing an effective online marketing campaign.

1. Clearly define your target audience and goals: Understand who you want to reach and what you want to achieve with your campaign.

2. Research your competitors and industry trends: Analyze what your competitors are doing and identify industry trends to inform your strategy.

3. Create a content strategy: Develop a plan for creating and distributing valuable and relevant content.

4. Optimize your website for search engines: Ensure that your website is optimized for search engines to improve your visibility and drive more traffic.

5. Use a mix of online channels: Utilize a variety of online channels, such as social media, email marketing, and pay-per-click (PPC) advertising, to reach your target audience.

6. Use analytics to track and measure the success of your campaigns: Use analytics tools to track the performance of your campaigns and measure the success of your efforts.

7. Test, refine, and adjust your strategies as needed: Regularly test different elements of your campaigns and make adjustments to improve their performance.

8. Be consistent and persistent in your efforts: Consistency and persistence are key to the success of any online marketing campaign. Keep at it and do not give up easily.

9. Personalize your communication and tailor your message to your audience, it will help to increase the chances of conversions.

10. Use A/B testing, to test different versions of your message, subject lines, images and other elements to see which one generates more engagement.

8

Networking for Success: Building Connections to Grow Your Wealth

Networking is a crucial component of building wealth and achieving success in any industry. By connecting with the right people, you can gain access to valuable resources, opportunities, and information that can help you to grow your wealth and achieve your goals.

One of the most effective ways to network is through attending industry events and conferences. These events provide an opportunity to meet and connect with other professionals in your industry, as well as to learn about the latest trends and developments. By building relationships with other professionals, you can gain access to new business opportunities, mentorship, and valuable advice.

Another effective networking strategy is to join professional organizations and associations. These organizations provide a platform for networking and professional development, and can help you to stay informed about the latest trends and developments in your industry. They also provide opportunities to connect with other professionals and gain access to resources and information that can help you to grow your business.

Networking can also be done through social media platforms, such as LinkedIn, Twitter, and Facebook. These platforms provide a great way to connect with other professionals in your industry, and to share information and resources. By building a strong online presence and engaging with others in your industry, you can increase your visibility and credibility, and gain access to new business opportunities.

Networking also involves building relationships with potential investors, customers, and partners. Building trust and a professional relationship with these key players can lead to new opportunities for growth and investment.

One effective way to network is by volunteering to be a mentor or mentee. By mentoring others, you can help to develop the next generation of professionals in your industry, and by being mentored, you can gain valuable knowledge and insight from experienced professionals.

In summary, networking is a crucial component of building wealth and achieving success in any industry. By connecting with the right people, you can gain access to valuable resources, opportunities, and information that can help you to grow your wealth and achieve your goals. Attend industry events and conferences, join professional organizations and associations, use social media platforms, and focus on building relationships with potential investors, customers, and partners, and by being a mentor or mentee.

STOP: What have you learned so far? Use this section to jot down notes.

9

Building and Managing a Credit Score: Personal And Business

Having a good credit score is essential for achieving financial success. A good credit score can help you qualify for lower interest rates on loans and credit cards, making it easier and more affordable to borrow money. It can also impact your ability to rent an apartment, get a job, or get a cell phone plan.

In order to build and maintain a good credit score, there are several key steps you can take:

1. Understand the basics of credit scores: Learn about the different types of credit scores, such as FICO and VantageScore, and how they are calculated. Understand the factors that go into determining your credit score, including payment history, credit utilization, length of credit history, and types of credit.

2. Check your credit report: Review your credit report regularly to check for errors and disputes any errors you find with the credit bureau.

3. Manage your debt: Keep your credit card balances low and make sure to pay your bills on time. Late payments can have a negative impact on your credit score.

4. Diversify your credit: Having a mix of different types of credit, such as a mortgage, a car loan, and a credit card, can help improve your credit score.

5. Limit new credit applications: Each time you apply for credit, it can have a negative impact on your

credit score. Try to limit the number of new credit applications you make.

6. Keep old credit accounts open: Length of credit history is a factor in determining your credit score, so keeping old credit accounts open can be beneficial.

In this chapter, we will go into more detail about the steps you can take to build and maintain a good credit score. We will also discuss the common mistakes people make when it comes to credit and how to avoid them. By understanding the basics of credit scores and taking steps to manage your debt and improve your credit, you can achieve financial success by having a good credit score. We will also touch on business credit.

There are several common mistakes that people make when it comes to credit, which can negatively impact their credit score.

Here are a few mistakes to avoid:

1. Not paying bills on time: Late payments can have a significant negative impact on your credit score, so

it's important to make sure that you pay all of your bills on time, every time.

2. Maxing out credit cards: High credit utilization, or using a large percentage of your available credit, can also have a negative impact on your credit score. Try to keep your credit card balances low and below 30% of your credit limit.

3. Closing credit accounts: Closing old credit accounts can shorten your credit history, which can have a negative impact on your credit score. It's better to keep old credit accounts open, even if you're not using them.

4. Applying for too much credit at once: Each time you apply for credit, it can have a negative impact on your credit score. Try to limit the number of new credit applications you make.

5. Not reviewing your credit report: Not regularly reviewing your credit report can lead to errors and inaccuracies remaining on your credit report, which can negatively impact your credit score.

6. Not seeking help when needed: If you're struggling to manage your debt or improve your credit score, it's important to seek the help of a credit counseling agency. They can provide you with budgeting advice and help you create a plan to pay off your debt.

By avoiding these common mistakes and taking steps to manage your debt, maintain a low credit utilization and a good payment history, you can help improve and maintain a good credit score.

Business credit is a separate credit score that is assigned to a business, rather than an individual. This score is used by lenders, suppliers, and other businesses to assess the creditworthiness of a business.

Having a good business credit score is important for a variety of reasons, including:

1. Access to credit: A good business credit score can help a business qualify for lower interest rates on loans, credit cards, and other forms of financing.

2. Establishing vendor credit: Many suppliers and vendors will extend credit to businesses with a good credit score, which can help the business save cash and manage their cash flow.

3. Building credibility: A good business credit score can help establish a business as credible and trustworthy, which can help attract new customers and partners.

4. To build and maintain a good business credit score, there are a few steps that a business can take:

5. Separate personal and business credit: It's important to keep personal and business credit separate, as this can help ensure that the business has its own credit score.

6. Establish a business credit history: One of the best ways to establish a business credit history is to open a business credit card, and use it responsibly by paying off the balance on time.

7. Monitor your credit: Just like personal credit, it's important to regularly check and monitor your business credit score to ensure that there are no errors or inaccuracies that could negatively impact it.

8. Pay bills on time: Late payments can have a negative impact on your business credit score, so it's important to make sure that all bills are paid on time.

There are several benefits to using business credit:

1. Increased purchasing power: Business credit allows companies to purchase goods and services on credit, which can help to increase purchasing power and allow for growth and expansion.

2. Improved cash flow: Business credit can help to improve cash flow by allowing companies to purchase goods and services now and pay for them later. This can help to smooth out cash flow and reduce the need for large amounts of upfront capital.

3. Building credit history: Establishing a positive credit history for your business can help to increase the chances of getting approved for future loans, credit lines, and other financial products.

4. Separation of personal and business finances: Business credit allows for a separation of personal and business finances, which can help to protect personal assets in the event of business financial difficulties.

5. Improved credit terms: Establishing good business credit can help to qualify for better credit terms from suppliers, including discounts and extended payment terms.

6. Access to capital: Business credit can be used to access capital for business expenses such as inventory, equipment, and expansions.

7. Credit-based loyalty programs: Some companies offer special incentives or rewards for businesses that use their credit, such as cashback or rewards points.

In summary, business credit can provide a range of benefits including increased purchasing power, improved cash flow, building credit history, separate personal and business finances, improved credit terms, access to capital, and credit-based loyalty programs.

STOP: What have you learned so far? Use this section to jot down notes.

_____

_____

_____

_____

_____

_____

_____

_____

_____

_____

_____

_____

_____

_____

_____

_____

_____

_____

_____

_____

_____

_____

10

Retirement Planning: Securing Your Financial Future

Retirement planning is an essential aspect of achieving financial success. It involves creating a plan to ensure that you have enough money to live on during your retirement years.

One important aspect of retirement planning is to start saving early and consistently. This can be done through employer-sponsored retirement plans, such as 401(k)s or IRAs, or through personal savings and investment accounts. The earlier you start saving, the more time your money has to grow and compound.

Another important aspect is to have a clear understanding of how much money you will need in retirement, and how to budget for it. This will help you to create a savings and investment plan that is tailored to your specific needs.

Diversifying your investments is also key to retirement planning, it helps to spread the risk and increase the chances of achieving your retirement goals. This can include a mix of stocks, bonds, real estate, and other investment options.

It's also important to review and adjust your plan regularly as your goals, circumstances and the market change. Reviewing and updating your plan can help ensure that you stay on track to achieve your retirement goals.

In this chapter, we will discuss the importance of retirement planning, the different types of retirement plans available and the importance of diversification. We will also provide tips on how to create a retirement budget, and how to adjust your plan as your circumstances and goals change over time.

There are several different types of retirement plans available, including:

1. 401(k) plans: A 401(k) plan is a tax-advantaged savings plan offered by many employers. Employees can contribute a portion of their salary to the plan,

and the funds grow tax-free until they are withdrawn. Employers may also make contributions to the plan.

2. Traditional IRA: A traditional IRA is an individual retirement account that allows individuals to make tax-deductible contributions and the funds grow tax-deferred until they are withdrawn.

3. Roth IRA: A Roth IRA is an individual retirement account that allows individuals to make contributions with after-tax dollars. The funds grow tax-free and can be withdrawn tax-free in retirement.

4. SEP IRA: A Simplified Employee Pension (SEP) IRA is a retirement plan for self-employed individuals or small business owners. It allows for tax-deductible contributions and tax-deferred growth.

5. Simple IRA: A Savings Incentive Match Plan for Employees (SIMPLE) IRA is a retirement plan for small businesses. It allows for employee contributions and employer matching contributions.

6. Pension plans: A pension plan is a retirement plan offered by some employers. It pays a fixed income to retirees, typically based on the employee's salary and years of service.

It's important to diversify your retirement investments to reduce risk. Diversifying means allocating your money across different types of investments such as stocks, bonds, real estate, and cash. It's also important to diversify within each type of investment. For example, if you're investing in stocks, invest in a mix of small-cap, mid-cap, and large-cap stocks, and across different sectors. Additionally, having a mix of pre-tax and after-tax accounts can also provide diversification benefits.

Creating a retirement budget is an important step in planning for your future.

Here are some tips on how to create a retirement budget:

1. Assess your current expenses: Make a list of all your current expenses, including housing, transportation, food, insurance, and entertainment. This will give you a baseline for your retirement budget.

2. Estimate your future expenses: Think about how your expenses may change in retirement. For

example, you may have less need for transportation costs, but you may have more healthcare expenses.

3. Consider your income sources: Determine how much income you will have in retirement from sources such as Social Security, pension plans, investments, and rental income.

4. Create a budget: Use the information from steps 1-3 to create a budget for your retirement. Be sure to include both fixed and variable expenses and make sure your income is sufficient to cover your expenses.

5. Review and adjust your budget regularly: Your circumstances and goals may change over time, so it's important to review and adjust your budget regularly. This will ensure that your budget stays on track and that your retirement savings are on track to meet your goals.

6. Assess inflation: Inflation can affect your budget over time, so you should consider how inflation may

affect your budget and make adjustments accordingly.

7. Consider unexpected expenses: Emergencies and unexpected expenses can happen at any time, so it's important to have a cushion in your budget to cover these unexpected expenses.

8. Be realistic: Your retirement budget should be realistic and achievable, so don't overestimate your income or underestimate your expenses.

9. Get professional help: If you are having trouble creating your retirement budget or understanding your financial situation, consider getting professional help from a financial advisor or accountant.

In summary, creating a retirement budget is an important step in planning for your future. Assessing your current expenses, estimating your future expenses, considering your income sources, creating a budget, reviewing and adjusting your budget regularly, assessing inflation, considering unexpected expenses, being realistic and getting professional help are some of the ways to create a successful retirement budget.

11

Building a Strong Financial Foundation

Building a strong financial foundation is crucial for achieving financial stability and reaching your financial goals.

Here are some key steps to building a strong financial foundation:

1. Create a budget: A budget is a crucial tool for managing your money and staying on track with your financial goals. It allows you to track your income and expenses, identify areas where you can cut back,

and make sure you have enough money to cover your bills and save for the future.

2. Establish an emergency fund: An emergency fund is a savings account set aside for unexpected expenses. It helps to ensure that you have enough money to cover unexpected expenses without having to rely on credit cards or loans. A general rule of thumb is to have 3-6 months of living expenses saved in an emergency fund.

3. Pay off debt: High levels of debt can be a major obstacle to achieving financial stability. Prioritize paying off high-interest debt, such as credit card debt, as quickly as possible.

4. Build a savings plan: Saving for the future is essential for achieving financial stability. Set savings goals for short-term and long-term expenses, such as retirement and college education.

5. Invest in your future: Investing is a key component of building wealth. Consider investing in a

diversified portfolio of stocks, bonds, and mutual funds to grow your money over time.

6. Get professional advice: Consider seeking the advice of a financial advisor to help you create a comprehensive financial plan and make informed investment decisions.

7. Protect your assets: Make sure you have adequate insurance to protect yourself, your family, and your assets in the event of an unexpected event.

8. Continuously educate yourself: Stay informed about financial matters by reading financial literature, attending seminars and workshops and keeping up with financial news.

Building a strong financial foundation takes time and effort, but it is a crucial step to achieving financial stability and reaching your financial goals. By creating a budget, establishing an emergency fund, paying off debt, building a savings plan, investing in your future, getting professional advice, protecting your assets and continuously educating yourself, you can take control of your finances and build a secure financial future.

12

Conclusion:

Putting it All Together and Staying on Track for Financial Success.

Achieving financial success is not a one-time event, but rather a continuous process that requires ongoing effort and discipline. Staying on track and maintaining financial success involves regularly reviewing and adjusting your financial plan, monitoring your progress, and staying focused on your goals.

One important aspect of staying on track is to regularly review and adjust your budget. As your income and expenses change over time, it's important to make sure that your budget remains realistic and reflects your current financial situation.

Another important aspect is to regularly review and monitor your investments. This includes staying informed about the current market conditions and making adjustments to your investment portfolio as needed.

It's also important to have a plan for dealing with unexpected expenses, such as a medical emergency or a job loss. An emergency fund can help to provide financial stability in times of unexpected need.

Additionally, it's important to stay focused on your long-term financial goals and to make sure that your daily spending and financial decisions align with those goals.

In this chapter, we will discuss the importance of staying on track and maintaining financial success. We will provide tips and strategies for regularly reviewing and adjusting your financial plan, monitoring your progress, and staying focused on your long-term goals. We will also discuss the importance of being prepared for unexpected events and how to handle them to keep your finances on track.

Here are some tips and strategies for regularly reviewing and adjusting your financial plan, monitoring your progress, and staying focused on your long-term goals:

1. Review your plan regularly: Review your financial plan at least once a year, and more often if you experience a significant change in your circumstances. This will help you to stay on track

with your goals and make any necessary adjustments.

2. Track your progress: Monitor your progress towards your financial goals by tracking your income, expenses, savings, and investments. This will help you to identify areas where you are making progress and areas where you need to make changes.

3. Set realistic and achievable goals: Set goals that are realistic and achievable, and make sure that your plan is aligned with your goals.

4. Be flexible: Be open to adjusting your plan as needed. Your circumstances and goals may change over time, so it's important to be flexible and make changes as needed.

5. Automate your savings: Automating your savings can help to ensure that you are saving regularly and consistently.

6. Stay focused on your long-term goals: It can be easy to get sidetracked by short-term financial issues, but it's important to stay focused on your long-term financial goals.

7. Make use of technology: Use technology to track your expenses, monitor your investments, and set reminders for important financial tasks.

8. Get professional advice: Consult a financial advisor regularly to help you review your plan, monitor your progress and make any necessary adjustments.

Remember that financial planning is a process, and you may encounter setbacks along the way. Don't be too hard on yourself if you encounter setbacks. Instead, learn from them and adjust your plan accordingly.

Being prepared for unexpected events is crucial for maintaining financial stability and achieving your financial goals. Unexpected events such as job loss, medical emergencies, or natural disasters can have a significant impact on your finances.

Here are some strategies for handling unexpected events to keep your finances on track:

1. Have an emergency fund: Having an emergency fund is a key strategy for handling unexpected events. It is a savings account set aside for unexpected expenses. It helps to ensure that you have enough money to cover unexpected expenses without having to rely on credit cards or loans. A general rule of thumb is to have 3-6 months of living expenses saved in an emergency fund.

2. Have adequate insurance: Make sure you have adequate insurance to protect yourself, your family, and your assets in the event of an unexpected event. This includes health insurance, life insurance, and property insurance.

3. Create a budget: A budget is a crucial tool for managing your money and staying on track with your financial goals. It allows you to track your income and expenses, identify areas where you can cut back, and make sure you have enough money to cover your bills and save for the future.

4. Have a plan for job loss: Job loss can be a major setback for your finances, so it's important to have a plan in place to handle this situation. This might include having a well-stocked emergency fund, networking to find a new job, and having a plan to generate income from other sources.

5. Be aware of government assistance: Be aware of government assistance programs that may be available to you in the event of an unexpected event.

6. Have a plan for natural disasters: Natural disasters can cause significant damage to your property and disrupt your finances. It's important to have a plan in place to handle this situation, such as having insurance, having an emergency fund, and knowing how to access government assistance.

7. Stay calm and take action: Unexpected events can be stressful, but it's important to stay calm and take action to address the situation. Take the time to assess the situation, gather information, and make a plan to address it.

In summary, being prepared for unexpected events is crucial for maintaining financial stability and achieving your financial goals. Having an emergency fund, adequate insurance, creating a budget, having a plan for job loss, being aware of government assistance, having a plan for natural disasters and staying calm and taking action are some ways to handle unexpected events and keep your finances on track.

STOP: What have you learned so far? Use this section to jot down notes.

13

BONUS

10 Side Hustles That You Can Turn Into Businesses

1. Online tutoring or teaching: You can use your expertise in a particular subject to teach or tutor students online.

2. Freelancing: Offer your services as a freelancer in areas such as writing, graphic design, or web development.

3. E-commerce: Start an online store and sell products or services through platforms like Amazon, Etsy, or your own website.

4. Consulting: Offer your expertise in a specific field to businesses or individuals who need it.

5. Pet-sitting or dog-walking: Starting your own pet-sitting or dog-walking business can be a great way to earn money while spending time with animals.

6. Home cleaning or organizing: Offer home cleaning or organizing services to busy individuals or families.

7. Event planning or coordination: Utilize your organizational skills to plan and coordinate events for clients.

8. Personal shopping or styling: Offer personal shopping or styling services to help people improve their personal style.

9. Social media management: Offer social media management services to businesses or individuals who want to improve their online presence.

10. Photography or videography: Use your photography or videography skills to shoot events, weddings, or create content for businesses.

These are some examples of side hustles that you can turn into businesses. With the right approach, hard work, and determination, you can turn your passion into a profitable business.

** Oh Don't forget about Uber, Lyft, and Door dash**

STOP: What have you learned so far? Use this section to jot down notes.

WANT A KICKSTART TO EARNING MORE MONEY? THIS IS A BOOK THAT WILL PAY YOU. SCAN THE QR CODE AND GO TO THE MONEY MAKER CHALLENGE LINK. ENTER CODE: 1224MMC

"The Wealth Code: Unlocking the Secrets to Making Money"

Meet Jasmine Dudley, a dynamic and accomplished business coach with over 10 years of experience in the industry. Jasmine is dedicated to helping entrepreneurs and business owners reach their full potential and achieve success in their ventures. She has a proven track record of guiding businesses to reach their goals, whether it's scaling their operations, increasing revenue, improving their leadership skills, or smoothly integrating new technologies.

Jasmine's coaching style is empowering, supportive and solution-focused. She works closely with her clients to understand their unique needs and goals, and provides them with the tools and resources they need to achieve success. Her clients appreciate her ability to understand their concerns, and provide them with the guidance and encouragement they need to overcome obstacles and reach their full potential.

Jasmine Dudley is also the Co-Founder and active CEO of Naomi's Connect Technology, DP House Publishers, and the 818 Wealth Academy. Born in Atlanta, Georgia, Mrs. Dudley has always had a passion for technology and its potential to change lives. After deciding college was not for her, she left and began working for a number of companies before co-founding her own publishing company in 2016. For over ten years, Mrs. Dudley has worked in the background of technology at various companies—including hers—specifically web, mobile, and software sales and development. In her current position at Naomi's Connect Technology, she helps to develop products that make it easier for people to connect with one another and share information.

As the CEO of the Naomi's Connect Technology, DP House, and 818 Wealth Academy brands she is responsible for strategic planning and growth, research, portfolio management, and many other aspects of the businesses. She has successfully overseen the expansion of all companies, increasing revenues and profits while maintaining a commitment to quality and customer satisfaction. In addition to her business acumen, she is also a highly skilled communicator and motivator, able to inspire and lead her team to achieve great things. She is truly a leader in every sense of the word, and under her guidance, both all of the companies that she leads are sure to continue to thrive.

She is an app developer of the groundbreaking trademarked and patented Naomi's Connect app that connects motherless daughters to daughterless mothers around the world. The app provides a forum for users to share their experiences, offer advice, and support one another as family. In addition, the app includes a directory of resources for motherless daughters and those who form mother-daughter relationships within the app, including books, articles, adult adoption information, counseling services, cookbook recipes, and motivational audios for daughters, and more. Users can also search for motherless daughters in their area and connect with them offline.

As a business consultant, Mrs. Dudley has a lot of experience helping companies grow and scale. However, she finds that her most successful clients are those who are already established and have been in business for a while. They usually come to her because they want to take their business to the next level and start making 6-8 figure profit months. These clients are usually very goal-oriented and driven, and they are willing to do whatever it takes to achieve their objectives. Mrs. Dudley enjoys working with them because she knows that they have the potential to be truly successful. She is able to provide them with the tools and resources they need to take their business to the next level. With her help, they are able to achieve their goals and reach new heights of success.

Mrs. Dudley is also an active investor and advisor to several early-stage technology companies and other businesses that agree with the landscape of her business portfolio.

In a world where the nine-to-five work week is increasingly becoming a thing of the past, it's no surprise that more and more people are turning to entrepreneurship to make a living. And among this new generation of entrepreneurs, one woman is making waves for her innovative approach to wealth generation. Dubbed the "Harriet Tubman of her generation," she is quickly becoming known as a millennial creative who is leading the charge when it comes to financial freedom. What sets her apart from other business leaders is her focus on creating multiple streams of income using technology, instead of relying on one source of income and manual labor. This not only provides financial stability in an unpredictable economic climate, but it also gives her the freedom to pursue her passion projects without worrying about money. As more and more people are struggling to make ends meet, she is proving that it is possible to create your own success story. And in doing so, she is inspiring a new generation of entrepreneurs to do the same.

Stay Connected to Coach Jasmine!

"The Wealth Code: Unlocking the Secrets to Making Money"

Extra Notes:

"The Wealth Code: Unlocking the Secrets to Making Money"

www.ingramcontent.com/pod-product-compliance
Lightning Source LLC
Chambersburg PA
CBHW071505200326

41519CB00019B/5874